MW00445279

Name: ______________________________

KINDERGARTEN
n o t e b o o k

Primary Lined Journal & Dot Grid

schoolnest

ART + BOOKS + NATURE

FIRST EDITION

www.theschoolnest.com

/ /

/ /

/ /

/ /

/ /

/ /

/ /

/ /

/ /

Made in the USA
Las Vegas, NV
13 January 2022

41260891R00111